Understanding Fours

Four-year-old children are learning to become social, both with adults and other children. They are energetic and imaginative and may confuse "make believe" with reality. They have also acquired many of the physical skills required to take care of most of their personal needs, such as brushing teeth, combing hair, and putting away belongings. Four year olds are eager learners and learn best when given the opportunity to do things for themselves and try new things.

- **Interaction**—Children at this age enjoy playing and talking with other children as well as seeking approval and praise from adults. Peer groups are becoming important, and group play often takes precedence over solitary time with toys. Four year olds are realizing the importance of sharing and cooperation in getting along with other people, and enjoy simple games, both structured and spontaneous. They are able to follow simple rules and can take turns and share with others. Four year olds can sometimes be bossy, and may need extra encouragement and support when disagreements arise with other children.

- **Creativity**—Four year olds often create situations and act them out. They enjoy role-playing important adults, such as parents, teachers, etc. Pretending helps children become more flexible in finding ways to deal with real-life situations. Teachers can encourage pretending by placing a variety of props in classroom centers, and initiating activities that involve dramatic play. Settings for role-playing can include a police or fire station, classroom, or grocery store.

- **Activity**—Four year olds are energetic and are proficient at any number of gross motor skills, including running, skipping, riding a tricycle, throwing, bouncing and catching a ball, and climbing on playground equipment. They also have longer attention spans, and can work on an activity until it is complete.

- **Language Skills**—Four year olds usually have good conversation skills, and can talk easily and without prompting. They are beginning to play with language, making up nonsense words and nicknames. Children at this age like to make up and tell jokes that may not make sense to adults. They will speak in complex sentences to adults, but tend to simplify their language when speaking to younger children. Four-year-old children are curious, and will often ask "Why?" and "How?"

Classroom Centers

Because four year olds are becoming increasingly social and less dependent on adults, it is important to provide them with opportunities to choose their own activities. Setting up a variety of classroom centers ensures that children will participate in different kinds of play of their own choosing each day.

Centers also provide a way to encourage children to keep materials organized. Make sure that the children know what items belong in which centers. You may wish to let the children turn clean-up time into a game by letting them name where different items belong, and then having the children replace the items in the correct centers.

• **Home Living Center**—Provide safe, child-sized furniture such as a table with chairs, a stove, oven, and refrigerator. Also include child-safe dishes, pots, pans, dolls, puppets, cradles, feather dusters, and brooms. Have older children's clothing available for them to dress in (adult clothing is often too large for young children). Provide props that will enable children to role play different community workers, family members, animals, etc. Occasionally place prop boxes in the center with additional items for the children to use. For example, a prop box for a grocery store could include aprons, paper bags, toy food, food packaging such as cereal boxes and clean, empty milk cartons, writing pads on which grocery lists can be written, and a toy cash register. Change the prop boxes when you want to add variety to this center.

Introduction

- **Block Center**—Have several low shelves containing blocks of various sizes and shapes. Encourage children to use the blocks in a carpeted area so that they do not disturb other children. You may wish to hang pictures of different kinds of structures in this area so the children will build similar structures. Get the children to talk about what they are building to improve their verbal skills.

- **Art Center**—Keep a variety of art materials at the center, such as blunt scissors, colored paper, crayons, markers, chalk, play clay, lace, ric rac, glue, sequins, and glitter. Also provide paint and an easel as often as possible. Allow the children time to explore these activities and create whatever they like.

- **Manipulative Center**—Provide materials, such as large beads, jigsaw puzzles, lacing cards and pegboards, to help develop fine motor skills as well as counting, and sequencing skills.

- **Book Center**—This area should have selection of age-appropriate books, as well as pillows, carpet squares, child-sized chairs, and stuffed animals, to encourage children to participate in quiet reading as well as storytelling. Four year olds enjoy silly stories and stories about adventures and pretend creatures, such as giants and fairies.

- **Gross Motor Center**—Set up climbing apparatuses, trucks, cars, and wagons in an open area for the children to use. Be sure that children play in this center in small, adult-supervised groups.

- **Writing Center**—To increase children's confidence in their writing, place paper, crayons, markers, and large pencils in this area. Encourage them to write and copy letters, numbers, and their names, and to draw and label pictures. Also have them write letters and hand-deliver them to their families. If possible, provide a computer keyboard or a typewriter and allow them to practice typing.

- **Science Center**—In this center, include various items that can be taken apart and put back together, objects from nature such as bird nests or large sea shells, and items with which the children can experiment, such as knobs or latches. Plan to perform simple experiments with the children, such as looking through a magnifying glass at leaves or watching a caterpillar make a cocoon.

- **Sand and Water Center**—Provide a sensory table filled with sand or water. Supply bathtub toys and tools for scooping, pouring, funneling, and measuring.

Planning Sheets

Curriculum Planning Sheet

Use the Curriculum Planning Sheet on pages 5–6 to help you organize specific units or themes. List on the sheet the specific skills you wish to focus on and reinforce. The sheet has space for you to include books or stories, language skills, art experiences, dramatic play, music/movement activities, indoor/outdoor games, science activities, and food experiences. Copy these sheets and use them as a reference when planning units year to year.

Weekly Planning Sheet

Use the Weekly Planning Sheet on page 7 to help you organize and plan activities on a weekly basis. Any activities that relate to a particular unit or holiday you are teaching during a particular week should be included.

Yearly Planning Sheet

The Yearly Planning Sheet on page 8 can be used to help you plan the units and themes you wish to cover throughout the year. Use the "Materials Needed" section to write down any additional materials you may need to acquire before beginning the unit.

Curriculum Planning Sheet

Unit Title: _____

Skills to Reinforce:

1. _____

2. _____

Books or Stories:

1. _____

2. _____

Language Skills:

1. _____

2. _____

Art Experiences:

1. _____

2. _____

Dramatic Play:

1. _____

2. _____

Curriculum Planning Sheet

Music/Movement:

1. _____

2. _____

Indoor/Outdoor Games:

1. _____

2. _____

Science Activities:

1. _____

2. _____

Math Activities:

1. _____

2. _____

Food Experiences:

1. _____

2. _____

Planning Sheets

Weekly Planning Sheet   Theme: _____   Week of: _____

Activity	Monday	Tuesday	Wednesday	Thursday	Friday
Books or Stories					
Language Skills					
Art Experiences					
Dramatic Play					
Music/Movement					
Indoor/Outdoor					
Science Activities					
Math Activities					
Food Experiences					

Yearly Planning Sheet

Month	Units or Themes		Materials Needed
September			
October			
November			
December			
January			
February			
March			
April			
May			
June			
July			
August			

Planning Sheets

Fall

Fall Celebrations

 Welcome Fall

Have the children help you make a list of all the fall celebrations they can think of. Some examples might be: Columbus Day, harvest, Halloween, or Thanksgiving. You may also want to share one of the literature selections from page 11. Provide paper and paint, crayons, or markers. Have each child think of his favorite thing to do in the fall, such as jumping in leaves, picking apples, or eating Halloween candy, and paint or draw a picture of himself doing that activity. Let each child dictate a sentence about his painting. Post the pictures on a bulletin board titled "Fall Fun."

 Flash Light Shadows

Make one copy of the Halloween cat and bat patterns from page 12 for each child. Have the children cut out the patterns. Have each child use masking tape to attach her patterns to the ends of two plastic drinking straws or craft sticks. Hold a flashlight or place an overhead projector in front of a large piece of white butcher paper that has been taped to the wall, or a white sheet that has been hung from a clothesline. Darken the room and have the children move the patterns in front of the flashlight or projector.

Feed the Jack-o'-lantern

Cut jack-o'-lantern features into a large, cardboard box. Make a hole for the mouth that is large enough to put your hand through. Cut 13 index cards in half, and write a letter on each one. Place these in a bag or basket. Have the children recite the following chant along with you.

I'm a big hungry jack-o'-lantern,
Orange and round.
I am sitting on the hard, cold ground.
Letters, letters are what I eat.
Feed me, feed me, a tasty treat!

Allow a child to pull a letter card out of the bag. Ask the child to say the name of the letter and then show it to the class. Have the child drop the card into the jack-o'-lantern's mouth. Continue playing until each child has a turn.

 Turkey Feathers

Give each child a copy of the turkey pattern from page 12. Have him cut it out, and then let him cover his turkey with white glue. Provide craft feathers in several different fall colors. Have the child place the feathers on his turkey. Let the turkey dry completely, then help the child gently shake the turkey over a large sheet of paper to remove any excess feathers so that they can be reused.

 Native American Headbands

Explain to the children that, although Native Americans dress in modern clothing, they still wear traditional costumes for special ceremonies. Cut an oaktag strip for each child that is about 18" x 2" wide. Have the children decorate the headbands using crayons, markers, glitter, and sequins. Tape the ends of the headband together to fit each child's head.

Fall: Fall Celebrations

Observing Popcorn Kernels

Explain to the class that Native Americans and Pilgrims shared popcorn as part of the first Thanksgiving. Bring in some unpopped kernels, and, if possible, some popcorn still on the cob. Let the children examine the popcorn, making sure they understand not to eat the corn. Pop some corn and let the children compare it to the unpopped kernels. You may wish to read *The Popcorn Book* by Tomie De Paola.

 Harvest Snack

Make a colorful harvest snack. You will need:

1/3 cup plus 1 tablespoon butter or margerine
10 1/2 ounce bag marshmallows
5 1/2 cups puffed rice cereal
1/4 cup dried apricots, finely chopped
6 ounces candy-coated chocolates
Large bowl
Large, heavy spoon
13" x 9" x 2" baking pan
Spatula

Use the 1 tablespoon of butter to grease the baking pan. Place the butter and marshmallows in the bowl. Heat in a microwave on high for two minutes, stirring occasionally (you may also heat butter and marshmallows over low heat in a saucepan). Let the children help you add the rice cereal, apricots, and candies, and then stir the mixture thoroughly. Press the mixture into a pan and allow it to cool partially. When the mixture is firm but still warm, cut it into squares. Insert a craft stick into each square. When the mixture is completely cool, remove the squares with a spatula and serve.

 Books to Share

Fall is Here! I Love It! by Elaine W. Good (Good Books, 1990)

The Popcorn Book by Tomie De Paola (Holiday House, 1989)

Red Leaf, Yellow Leaf by Lois Ehrert (Harcourt Brace, 1991)

Sarah Morton's Day, A Day in the Life of a Pilgrim Girl by Kate Waters (Scholastic, 1993)

Turkey, Cat, and Bat Patterns

Fall: Fall Celebrations © Carson-Dellosa CD-0217

My Family and Me

 Family Class Book

Give the children an opportunity to describe some of their family activities, traditions, gatherings, and family trips. You may wish to share the book *All Kinds of Families* by Norma Simon. Supply paper, markers and crayons so that each child may draw a picture of her family. Allow the children to name their family members while you label them. Combine the pictures in a class book.

 Classroom Props

Provide play items that depict family life. Place pictures of different kinds of homes in the block center to encourage the children to make block structures that look like the homes. Place pots and pans, family dolls and cleaning items in the home living center to encourage family play. In the book center be sure to have lots of books about families (see the literature list on page 15 for suggestions).

 Family Photographs

Ask parents to send in small family photographs. Provide each child with an 8" x 8" square piece of construction paper, and a triangular piece of construction paper with one 8" side. Have each child glue the triangle to the top of the square to form the shape of a house. Have each child draw a door shape on each square large enough to expose the whole photograph. Help each child cut the right side and top of the door, then fold the cut-out piece over to resemble an open door. Help each child tape or glue the family photograph to a sheet of construction paper, then glue the house over it so that the photograph shows through the open door. Then, let him decorate his house. Place a bulletin-board-sized piece of butcher paper on the floor or a table. Tape all of the houses to the paper, and let children add streets, trees, grass, clouds, etc. Attach the finished neighborhood to a bulletin board.

 **Family Members Do This**
Suggest that the children demonstrate something they see their fathers do. You could demonstrate first by pretending to put on a tie. Have the children guess what you are doing. Then, have the children take turns acting out shaving, brushing hair, etc. You may expand the activity by having the children act out something their mothers, sisters, brothers, or grandparents do.

 Letters Home
On one of the classroom tables or at the class writing center, provide different kinds of stationery, colored paper, envelopes, crayons, markers, and pencils. Encourage a few children at a time to come to the table and "write" letters to their families. Children may draw pictures, write their names and addresses, or dictate short letters. Let the children deliver the letters to their families.

 Funny Family Story
Start a story for all of the children, allowing each child to add to it. The story could begin like this: "One day, Alex's family went to his cousin's house for a visit. When they got there, Alex's aunt had a big surprise for him. It was a…" At this point, let another child add a sentence or two to the story. Encourage the child to build on the story by asking her questions, such as "What was the surprise? Where did they go next?" etc. Write each sentence on a piece of chart paper. Continue until each child has a chance to contribute to the story. Then, take the chart paper pages and combine them into a class book.

 Cookie Decorating
Designate a day where parents and grandparents are invited to help the children decorate cookies. Bring a batch of large sugar cookies to class. Provide tubes of colorful icing. (Make sure the children understand that they will put icing on after the cookies have baked and cooled.) Let the guests help the children decorate and eat the cookies. You may want to take pictures of this activity to display on the bulletin board.

Fall: My Family and Me

Parents at Work

Send a note to parents asking that they send pictures of themselves at work. Have parents write the names of their jobs on the backs of their photographs. Ask the parents to include some of the equipment that they use at work in the photographs. Share the pictures with the class, and have each child talk about what her parents do at work.

 Counting Family Members

On large squares of paper, write the numerals 1 through 10. Place these on the floor in different parts of the room. Have each child tell how many members he has in his family (make sure he counts himself). Each child should then stand next to the number of members in his family. To chart the findings, write the numerals 1 through 10 across a large piece of paper. Write each child's name under the numeral which indicates the number of family members he has. Count the names under each numeral and determine which number has the most children's names under it.

 Family Portraits

Give each child four 8½" horizontal strips of construction paper (any color). Have her glue these together at the corners to make a square picture frame. Let the child decorate her frame with sequins, glitter, stickers, paint, markers, and crayons. While the frames are drying, provide squares of paper approximately the same size as the frames, and paint or crayons and markers. Then, have each child draw pictures of his family members on the paper. Glue the family portraits so that they fit inside of the frames. Display these on a bulletin board. Encourage each child to tell about her family members.

 Books to Share

All Kinds of Families by Norma Simon (Albert Whitman and Co., 1987)

Big Sister, Little Sister by Charlotte Zolotow (HarperTrophy, 1990)

Daddy Makes the Best Spaghetti by Anna Grossnickle Hines (Clarion Books, 1988)

The Quilt Story by Tony Johnston (Putnam, 1985)

Squirrels and Nuts

 Sorting Acorns and Nuts

Explain to the children that squirrels are getting ready for the winter months by building nests and storing away food. You may want to share one of the literature selections about squirrels on page 18. Provide a variety of different kinds of nuts. Have the children sort the nuts by kinds and sizes. Encourage them to think of other ways the nuts could be sorted.

 Counting Nuts

Provide a number of unshelled nuts. With a permanent marker, write the numerals 0 through 10 on paper cups. Have the children fill each cup with the correct number of nuts.

 Acorn Painting

Have children place several acorns or other unshelled nuts in a small container of liquid tempera paint. Help the children use plastic spoons to transfer the nuts to paper which has been placed in the lid of a gift box. Let the children roll the nuts around in the box lid, making a variety of patterns on the paper. Let the paint dry completely, then remove the nuts. You may wish to reserve the colorful nuts to use as counters.

 Squirrel Puppets

Using a copy of the squirrel pattern from page 19, allow each child to cut out a squirrel from brown or gray construction paper. Cut out the two holes for the children's fingers. Glue a small acorn between the holes. Let the children place their fingers through the holes to make their squirrel puppets hold the nuts.

Fall: Squirrels and Nuts

🎵 Squirrel Song
Sing to the tune of "Old MacDonald."

Little squirrel runs on the ground, E-I-E-I-O!
A yummy acorn he has found, E-I-E-I-O!
He looks over here, and he looks over there!
He eats the nut and runs everywhere!
Little squirrel runs on the ground, E-I-E-I-O!

Crunchy Squirrel Snacks
Provide a variety of grain-type cereals which do not contain raisins or nuts. Give each child a paper cup and a plastic spoon. Let each child spoon out some of each of the dry ingredients and mix them together in her cup. When she is finished mixing the ingredients, let each child use her spoon to enjoy the squirrel snack.

Nut Sequencing
Copy the nut patterns from page 19 onto red, yellow, and blue construction paper. Let the children help cut out the patterns. Tie a clothesline between two chairs and furnish a supply of pinch-type clothespins. Start a pattern on the clothesline: one yellow nut, two red nuts, one yellow nut, two red nuts, etc. Have a child add the next piece to continue the pattern. Then, have each child start his own pattern, calling on another child to continue it.

Get Ready for Winter
Using brown construction paper, copy and cut out several of the nut patterns from page 19. Place the nuts around the room. Have the children pretend to be squirrels preparing for winter. Let them gather the nuts and pretend to bury (hide) them in desks and on the floor. To extend the play, have the children pretend it is now winter, and see how many of their hidden nuts they can find.

© Carson-Dellosa CD-0217   *Fall: Squirrels and Nuts*

Squirrel Movement Activity

Have children act out the movements as you recite the following phrases.

Acorn, acorn falling from the tree.
(*Move arms up and down to represent falling nuts.*)

Brown squirrel watching quiet as can be.
(*Squat and fold arms over chest like squirrel paws.*)

Tiptoe, tiptoe, little squirrel feet.
(*Stand and tiptoe around*)

Hurry! Hurry! Grab that treat!
(*Pretend to grab the nut and run.*)

 Nutty Drums

Provide a plastic food container with a lid, such as a margarine tub, for each child. Let each child place several unshelled nuts in the container. Help each child replace the lid. Play some lively music and let the children shake the tubs.

 Observing Real Squirrels

Place a gift box lid on a flat surface outside, but in sight of a classroom window. Place nuts, sunflower seeds, bread and peanut butter, or dry dog food in the box. Let the children go to the window and check the feeder throughout the day to see if any squirrels come to eat. You may wish to make a graph that lists the number of squirrels found at the feeder at different times throughout the day. Keep track of the graph for a week.

 Books to Share

Nuts to You by Lois Ehlert (Harcourt Brace, 1993)

Squirrels by Brian Wildsmith (Oxford University Press, 1984)

Fall: Squirrels and Nuts

Acorn and Squirrel Patterns

© Carson-Dellosa CD-0217   19   *Fall: Squirrels and Nuts*

Pumpkins

 Classroom Pumpkin Patch
Bring in several lunch-sized paper bags. Let the children paint the bags orange. Allow them to dry completely, then have each child draw a face on her pumpkin. Let each child stuff her bag with crumpled newspaper, and tie or rubber band the top closed. Have her paint the top green to resemble a stem. Place the bags around the classroom. Have children pretend to be skipping, hopping, and creeping through a pumpkin patch. Let each child "pick" her pumpkin to take home.

 Pumpkin Muffins
Let the children mix and eat muffins. You will need:

2 eggs, beaten
1 cup sugar
$1/3$ cup water
$1/2$ cup oil

1 cup canned pumpkin
$2^{3}/_{4}$ cups self-rising flour
1 teaspoon cinnamon

Mix all ingredients together thoroughly. Spray muffin tins with non-stick cooking spray, or line them with paper muffin holders. For large muffin tins, place two tablespoons of batter into each muffin cup. For small muffin tins, use one tablespoon of batter per muffin cup. Bake at 350° for 25 minutes. Let the muffins cool completely and then have each child enjoy a pumpkin treat!

 Tissue Paper Pumpkins
Using the large pumpkin pattern from page 23, let each child cut out a construction paper pumpkin shape. Cut sheets of orange tissue paper into 1" squares. Give each child some of the tissue paper squares to crumple. Let each child cover his pumpkin with white glue and then add crumpled tissue paper to make textured pumpkin art. Allow to dry completely.

Fall: Pumpkins

Pumpkins on a Fence

Teach location words using several copies of the small pumpkin patterns from page 23. Cut out three 1' strips and four 1½' strips of brown poster board. Arrange the strips on a bulletin board to make a split rail fence. Have children take turns placing a pumpkin on or around the fence as you give directions such as: "Put your pumpkin *on* the fence," "Place your pumpkin *beside* the fence," etc.

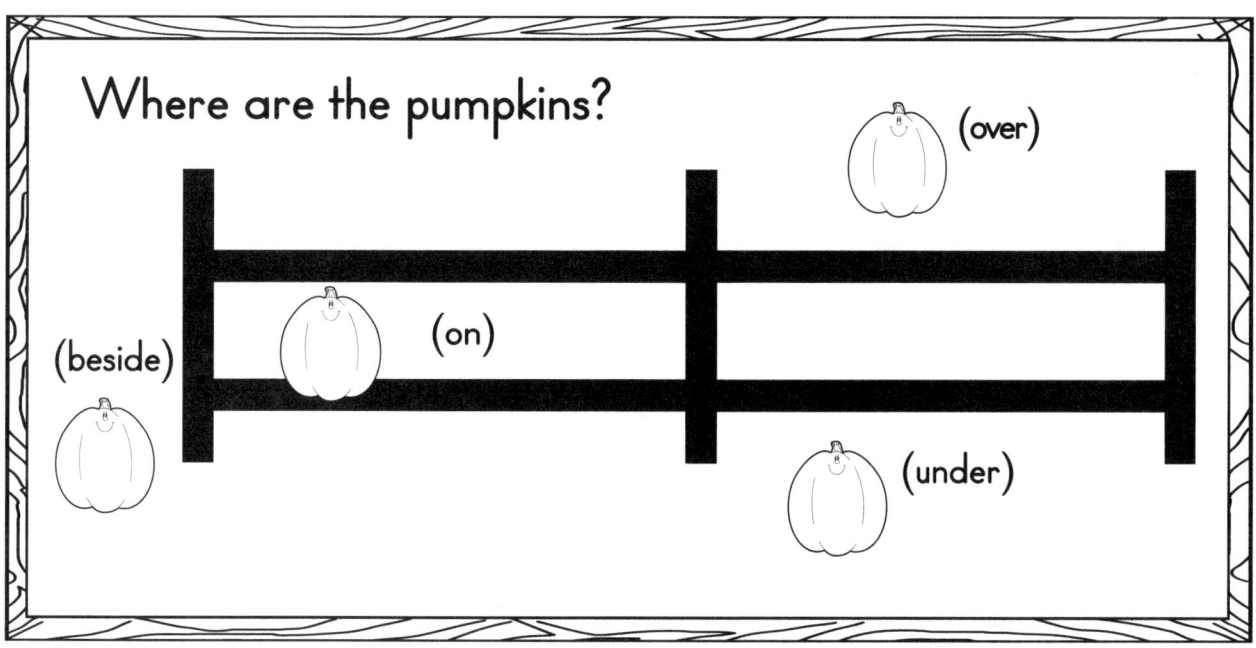

 Pumpkin, Pumpkin Chant

Have the children make the movements as you recite the following chant.

Pumpkin, pumpkin, orange and round.
(*Make arms into a circle.*)

Pumpkin, pumpkin sitting on the ground.
(*Squat down to the ground.*)

Farmer, farmer, look at me.
(*Point to self.*)

What a funny jack-o'-lantern I would be!
(*Jump up and spread arms wide and smile.*)

© Carson-Dellosa CD-0217   *Fall: Pumpkins*

Ten Little Pumpkins Finger Play

Copy one small pumpkin pattern from page 23 for each child to use as a finger puppet. Attach a strip of paper or tape to the back of each shape so that it will stay on the child's finger. Let ten children at a time use their pumpkins in the following finger play, which is sung to the tune of "Ten Little Indians."

One little, two little, three little pumpkins,
Four little, five little, six little pumpkins
Seven little, eight little, nine little pumpkins
Ten pumpkins sitting on the ground.

Have the children sit in a row on the floor. As you say each number, have one child hold up the pumpkin on her finger, and continue to hold it up as you add to the number of pumpkins in the song. Repeat the chant counting backwards, having the children lower their fingers as you decrease the number of pumpkins.

Pumpkin Patch

Provide a prop box containing items such as a straw hat, work gloves, children's overalls or work pants, and a heavy work shirt. Have the children take turns dressing up as farmers. Create a classroom pumpkin patch by placing several plastic pumpkins around the room. Encourage the children to pretend to plant, water, and harvest the pumpkins.

Pumpkin Seed Name Picture

Bring in a supply of clean, dry pumpkin seeds. Give each child a sheet of orange construction paper. Help each child write the first letter of his name using white glue. Then, let him place pumpkin seeds on the glue so that the letter appears in pumpkin seeds. As each child finishes covering one glue letter with seeds, help her write the next letter in her name or initials with the glue. Continue until each child has spelled her name in pumpkin seeds. Allow the names to dry.

Books to Share

The Biggest Pumpkin Ever by Steven Kroll (Cartwheel Books, 1993)

Pumpkin Pumpkin by Jeanne Titherington (Mulberry Books, 1990)

Fall: Pumpkins

Pumpkin Patterns

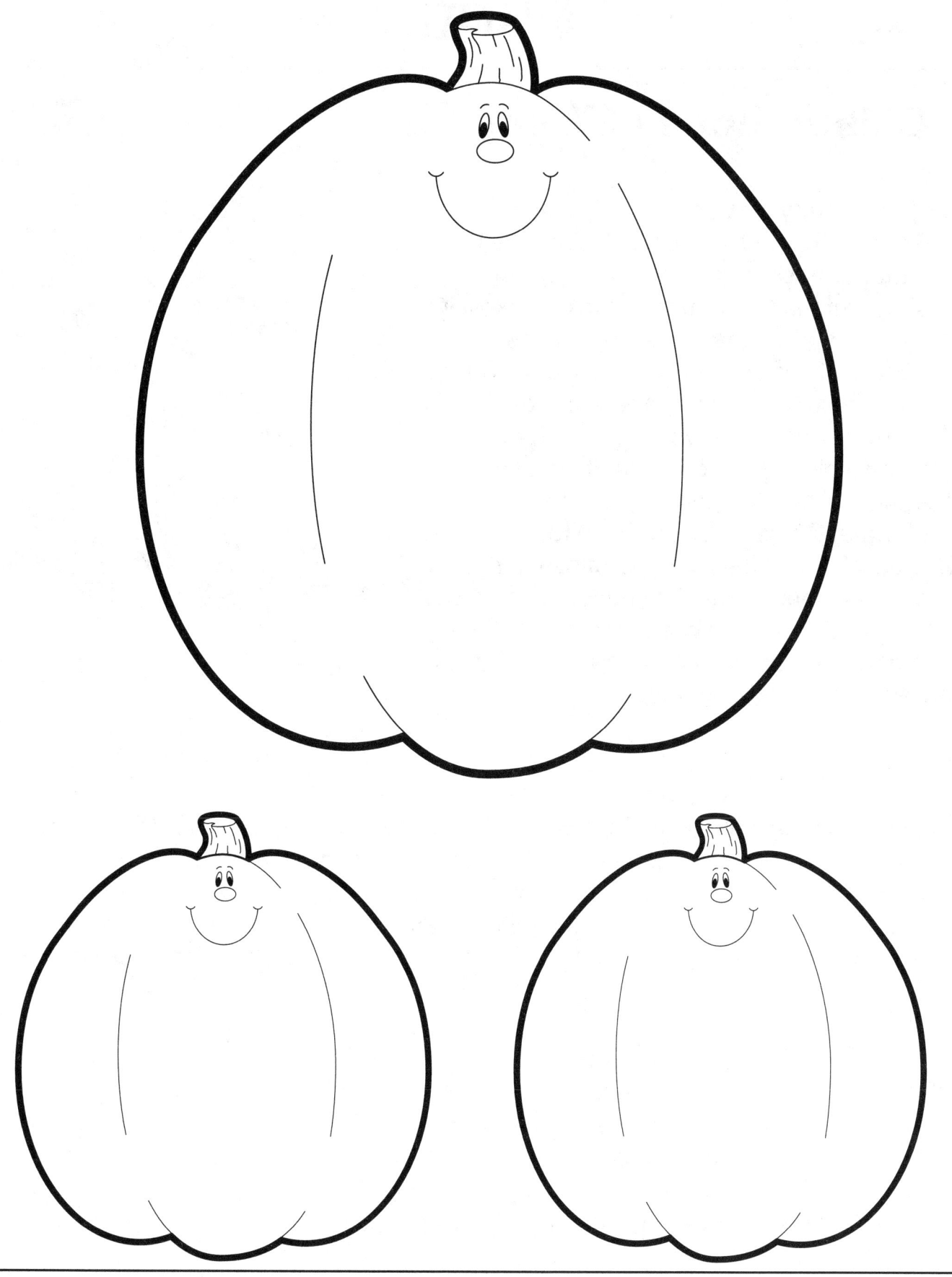

© Carson-Dellosa CD-0217　　　23　　　*Fall: Pumpkins*

Winter

Celebrations of Winter

 Candy Houses

Prior to this activity, collect pint-sized milk cartons, rinse them well, and tape the tops shut. Purchase pre-made icing or make icing by beating together three egg whites and 16 ounces of confectioner's sugar. Cover a classroom table with waxed paper. Give each child a milk carton and have him cover it with icing using a blunt, plastic knife or a craft stick. Let each child add graham crackers for roof shingles. Then, let each child cover his "house" with different types of candies, such as mints, gumdrops, and butterscotch drops (make sure the children do not eat these). When the icing has hardened, display all the houses on a table or tray.

 Wassail

Explain to the children that *wassail* is a hot spiced drink enjoyed at holiday time. To make wassail, let the children help put several cinnamon sticks and a few whole cloves into a tea ball or small cheesecloth bag. Put the bag into a pot of apple juice and stir. Heat until the juice is warm, but not hot. Then, ladle out the wassail into foam cups. Allow the drink to cool briefly before the children drink it.

 Stocking Decorations

Copy one stocking pattern from page 28 for each child. Punch a hole in the loop of each stocking and insert a yarn loop so that it can be hung from the ceiling, mantle, or a tree. Have the children cut out their stockings. Furnish a variety of materials for the children to use in decorating the stockings, such as ric rac, lace, pom-poms, cotton balls, buttons, fabric squares, tissue paper, glitter, etc.

Hanukkah Gelt Hunt

Explain to the children that *gelt* are coins hidden by Jewish parents for their children to find. Provide money manipulatives, chocolate foil money, or real money. Place different amounts of money into small bags (one per child), and hide these around the room. Tell the children to find one bag of coins. When the children have found the coins, let each child try to count how many coins are in his bag. Have each child replace the money in the bag and hide it for another child to find.

 "First Fruits" Buffet

The day before this activity, cover the snack table with a large piece of white butcher paper. Have the class create a Kwanzaa tablecloth by painting or coloring the butcher paper with red, green, and black paints or markers. Let the tablecloth dry overnight. Send a note to parents explaining the significance of Kwanzaa and the children's plans to share a bountiful harvest buffet. Ask each family to send something to be shared by the class, such as sliced grapes, baby carrots, banana circles, or peeled, chopped apple. Provide paper plates and napkins, and eat the feast on the Kwanzaa tablecloth.

 New Year Celebration

Explain to the children that celebrating the New Year is like celebrating a birthday, and that many people have parties for the occasion. Plan to have party food, such as cake and ice cream, for the first day of class in the New Year. Before the party, give each child a square piece of patterned wallpaper that will make a cone. Let each child shape the wallpaper into a cone to fit her head, then tape the edges together. Provide glue, stickers, glitter, pom-poms, and other materials for the children to decorate their hats. Let them wear their hats during the New Year's party.

© Carson-Dellosa CD-0217   Winter: Celebrations of Winter

Groundhog Puppets

Let each child cut out a copy of the groundhog pattern from page 28. Have the children tape their groundhogs to wooden craft sticks. Give each child a large paper or foam cup with a slit cut in the bottom. Help him put the craft stick through the slit, so that the groundhog is sticking out of the cup. Let the children practice pushing the groundhog out of his "hole." Use a flashlight to help make groundhog shadows on a wall or, if weather permits, go outside and see if the children can see the groundhogs' shadows on the ground.

 Look at Shadows

Take the children outside on a clear, sunny day. Have them look for their shadows. Then, go inside and dim the lights, or go out on a cloudy day. Have them try to find their shadows again. Explain that it must be bright for them to see a shadow. You may want to explain the legend of the groundhog looking for his shadow on Groundhog Day, February 2nd.

 Broken Heart Game

Bring a heart-shaped candy box to class. Using the heart patterns from page 28, copy and cut out 26 hearts using one color of construction paper. On one half of each heart, write an uppercase letter. On the other half, write the corresponding lowercase letter. Cut a jagged or curved line down the center of each heart. Give each child one heart half, making sure that another child has the corresponding heart half. For example, if you give one child an uppercase *A*, make sure another child has the lowercase *a*. Then, let the children try to find their matches.

Valentine Cards

Cut regular kitchen sponges in varying heart-shaped sizes or purchase heart-shaped sponges at a craft store. Use a hot glue gun to attach each heart to an empty sewing thread spool. This will serve as a handle when the children use the heart "stamps." To make a stamp pad, pour red tempera paint over a paper towel placed in a foam meat tray. Furnish white paper, and envelopes for children to stamp with the heart-shaped sponges to create cards for friends and family.

A Tisket, a Tasket, a Valentine Basket

Copy the heart patterns from page 28 onto red, white, and pink construction paper. Cut out the hearts, then on the back of each write a direction, such as *jump three times*, *crawl like a snake*, *flap your arms*, etc. Place all the hearts in a basket. Sing the following song, and at the end of the verse, let a child choose one of the hearts and perform the activity. Allow each child to have a turn.

A tisket, a tasket, a valentine basket,
I took a valentine to my friend and this
is what he did.

 Books to Share

The Christmas Star by Marcus Pfister (North South Books, 1997)

It's Groundhog Day by Steven Kroll (Scholastic Trade, 1995)

My First Hanukkah Book by Aileen Fisher (Children's Press, 1985)

My First Kwanzaa Book by Deborah M. Newton Chocolate (Cartwheel Books, 1992)

One Very Best Valentine's Day by Joan W. Blos (Aladdin, 1998)

Stocking, Heart, and Groundhog Patterns

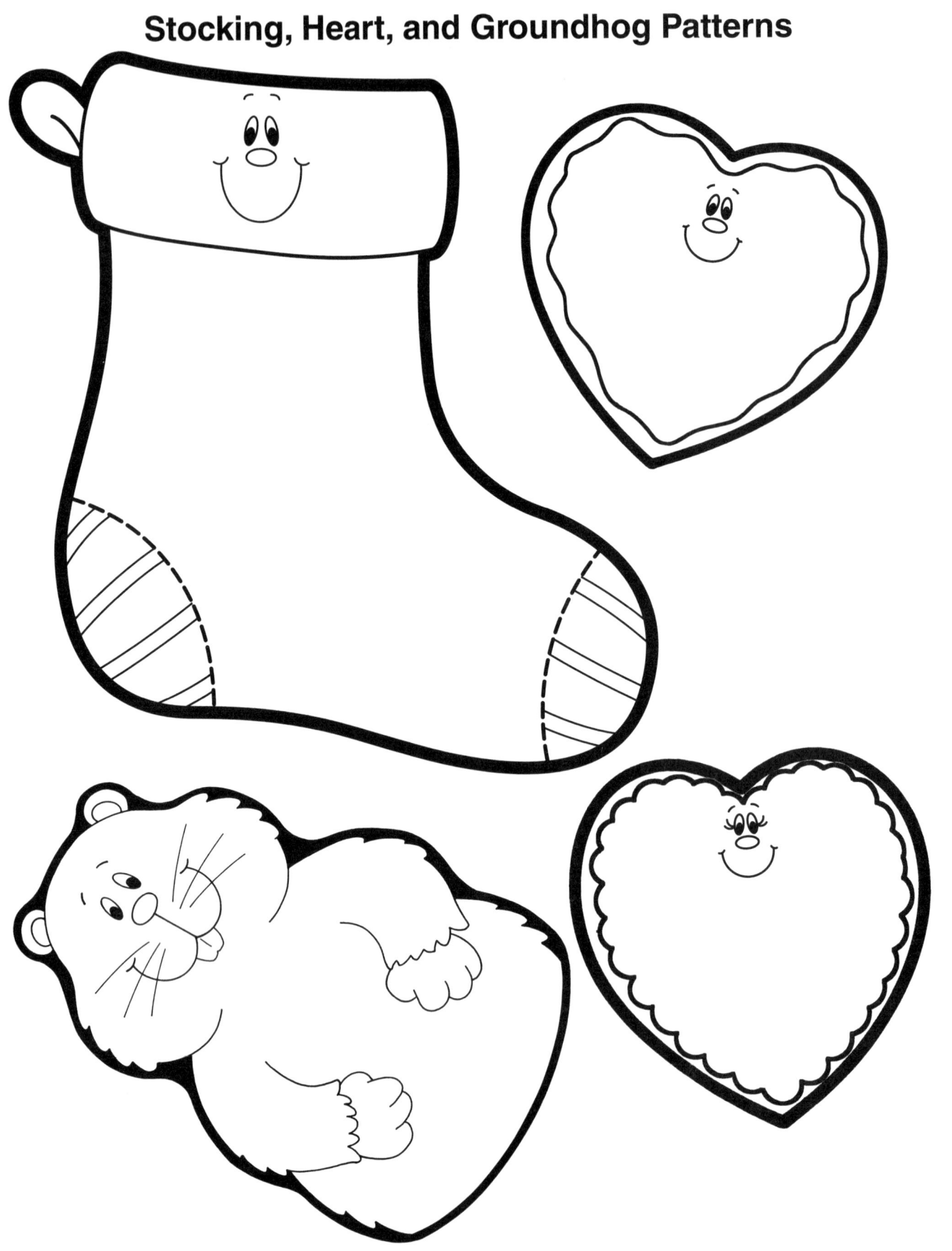

Winter: Celebrations of Winter 28 © Carson-Dellosa CD-0217

Bears

 All Kinds of Bears

Share the book *Bears in Pairs* by Niki Yektai. Show pictures of different kinds of bears: polar bears, black bears, brown bears, etc. Use a globe to show the children where each type of bear lives, what the weather there is like, etc. Talk about what most bears have in common. They all have fur, they are mammals, they all have four paws with claws, most of them grow to be large. Talk about what bears eat (fish, ants, fruits, nuts, plants). Copy one of the bear patterns from page 32 for each child. Let him color the bear to look like his favorite type of bear.

Hibernating Bears Bulletin Board

Share a book about hibernation, such as *Wake Me in Spring* by James Preller, or explain hibernation to the children. Prepare a bulletin board with blue paper on the top half to represent sky, and white paper on the bottom half to represent snow. Let the children glue white cotton to the bulletin board for more snow. In the middle of the board place a large semicircle of black paper, straight side down, to resemble a bear cave. Give each child a dessert-size paper plate. Let the children paint their paper plates with brown or black paint. After they are dry, have the children glue wiggly eyes and construction paper ears and mouths to the plates to make bear faces. Staple the bears in and around the cave.

 Building a Den

Tell the children that some bears create places to rest for the winter by making huge nests out of twigs, dried leaves, and moss. Take the class outside and help them gather some of these items. Inside, copy the bear pattern (standing on all fours) from page 32 for each child. Let each child cut out her bear pattern and glue her bear to a black sheet of construction paper. Have her glue twigs and leaves around the bear to make a den.

Polar Bear-cicles

Prepare a cold, tasty treat with the children. Mix 1 cup of mashed blueberries into 6 cups of vanilla yogurt. Have each child spoon some of the mixture into a small paper cup. Then, place a craft stick in the center. Freeze overnight. The next day, the children can peel away the cup and eat a "beary" delicious treat!

Sleeping Bear Song

Sing to the tune of "Where is Thumbkin?"
Have the children sing the song with you until they are familiar with it. Then, let the children take turns acting out the song. Let some children pretend to be the sleeping bears and let others tip toe to the bears' cave.

Are you sleeping? Are you sleeping?
Little bear, little bear.
Are you in your cave? Are you in your cave?
Where, oh, where? Where, oh, where?

Snoring. Snoring. Snoring. Snoring.
In the cave, in the cave.
Little bear is sleeping. Little bear is sleeping.
Let's be quiet. Let's be quiet.

Tip toe, tip toe. Tip toe, tip toe.
To the cave, to the cave.
Better not go inside. Better not go inside.
Let him sleep. Let him sleep.

Fuzzy Brown Bears

Let each child cut out a copy of one of the bear patterns from page 32. Provide each child with short lengths (1") of brown, black or white yarn, with each child choosing according to what kind of bear he prefers to make. Let each child cover his bear with yarn pieces. Let the fuzzy bears dry completely.

Winter: Bears   © Carson-Dellosa CD-0217

What Do You Hear?

Read Bill Martin's book, *Polar Bear, Polar Bear, What Do You Hear?* Then, sit quietly with the children and encourage them to listen to the sounds around them. Talk to the children about some of their favorite sounds. Do this activity outside and listen to the sounds of the day. If it is a really cold day in your area you may hear some sounds you would not hear on other days. Listen especially for wind, animal, and bird sounds.

 Where Is the Bear?

Bring in a small teddy bear. Place the bear in different places around the room. Each time you place the bear, have the children describe where the bear is, using a position word. The bear could be *on* the table, *under* a chair, etc.

 "Bear-achute" Teamwork

Bring a stuffed teddy bear and a large sheet or parachute to class. Take the children outside or into an open play area and have them stand in a circle. Spread the sheet on the ground in the middle of the circle and place the teddy bear in the middle. Have the children pick up the edges of the sheet and toss the teddy bear in the air. Explain to them that if anyone drops his part of the sheet, the teddy bear will fall to the ground, so they must all work together to keep the teddy bear bouncing in the air.

 Books to Share

Bears in Pairs by Niki Yektai (Aladdin Books, 1991)

Little Polar Bear by Hans de Beer (North South Books, 1989)

Polar Bear, Polar Bear, What Do You Hear? by Bill Martin (Henry Holt & Co., 1991)

Sleepy Bear by Lydia Dabcovich (E. P. Dutton, 1993)

The Winter Bear by Ruth Craft and Eric Blegvad (Aladdin Books, 1989)

Wake Me in Spring by James Preller (Cartwheel Books, 1994)

Bear Pattern

Winter: Bears 32 © Carson-Dellosa CD-0217

Games and Toys

 Toy Day
Designate a day for each child to bring in his favorite toy and show it to the class. Allow about five children per day to bring in toys. On the day that each child brings his toy, have him draw a picture of it. Help him label the picture. When all the children have drawn pictures of their favorite toys, combine the pictures into a class book. Display the toys on a special shelf for the day.

 Toy Collage
Bring in catalogs (especially from department stores) and magazines for the children to cut apart for making a cooperative collage of pictures of toys. Have the children cut or tear out pictures and glue them on a large piece of paper so that they overlap somewhat. Display the finished collage and have each child point to a favorite toy.

 I Spy
Cut out several pictures of toys from magazines and paste them onto a large sheet of paper or poster board, or use the collage from above. Glue pictures of items such as a red fire truck, yellow ball, blue tricycle, etc., randomly around the collage. Ask the children, "Who can spy a red fire truck on the collage?" Then, one at a time, name the other items you included for the children to find. You may want to let them take turns being the "spy."

 What Toy Am I?
Whisper the name of a toy in a child's ear. Then, let the child pretend to play with the toy, and let the other children guess what the toy is. Allow each child to have a turn.

© Carson-Dellosa CD-0217　　　　33　　　　*Winter: Games and Toys*

A Story of Toys
Using one of the classroom puppets or stuffed animals, start a story about the toy coming to life. Let the children take turns adding a sentence to the story. Write each child's sentence on a separate sheet of paper as he says it. At the end of the story, give each child the piece of paper with his sentence written on it, and ask him to illustrate his sentence. Display the illustrated story in chronological order on a bulletin board. For an added challenge, periodically take down the story pages and mix them up, letting a different child each time try to put the pages back into the correct sequence.

 Wind-Up Toys
Show the children some examples of toys that you must wind up to make them move. Have the children talk about the different movements. How are they the same? How are they different? Encourage them to use words like *fast* and *slow*. Then, pretend to wind up the children and watch them move. Have them move quickly and then slowly.

 Block Pattern Puzzles
Use a black marker to trace different blocks from the block area onto sheets of colorful construction paper. Laminate the sheets of construction paper, and then place the laminated paper in the Block Area. Let the children match up different blocks with their corresponding shapes.

 Sock Puppets
Furnish a supply of colored socks or ask each parent to send a clean, adult-size sock for the child to use. Ahead of time, if you wish, have a parent sew two buttons for eyes on the toe of each sock. To create sock puppets, have the children glue on shapes cut from felt and other fabrics, ricrac, lace, yarn, etc. The children can then use their puppets to put on puppet shows for the class.

Winter: Games and Toys

Graphing Toys

Glue several pictures of toys to the top of a piece of poster board. Use a hole punch to make a hole under each picture. Give each child a paper clip and have her attach a paper clip under her favorite toy so the clip hangs down. Let the rest of the children attach their paper clips to the hole or to the paper clips which are already attached. When all have participated, count the number of clips under each toy. Which toy is the most popular?

 Making Puzzles

Have each child make a watercolor picture of a toy he likes. Allow it to dry, then laminate it. Cut each child's picture into several pieces. Write the child's name or initials on the back of each piece of her puzzle to identify the puzzles. Store each puzzle in a resealable plastic bag. The children can enjoy putting their own puzzles together or they can switch and put a friend's puzzle together.

 Box Blocks

Ask parents to bring in a variety of boxes such as cereal boxes, round boxes, shoe boxes, etc. Put the boxes on a table. Use masking tape to tape the boxes closed if needed. Allow the children to build with the boxes. Encourage them to name and describe the structures they make.

 Ring Toss

Prior to class, use a utility knife to cut 1" circles from a round oatmeal container to make tossing rings. Cut a hole in a box or milk carton and insert a paper towel tube in the hole so that the tube stands vertically. Have the children stand a distance away and toss the circles onto the paper towel tube.

 Books to Share

Corduroy by Don Freeman (Scholastic, 1968)

My Toys by Lawrence DeFiori (Macmillan, 1983)

The Velveteen Rabbit by Margery Williams Blanco (Avon Books, 1975)

Winter Fun

 What We Wear in Winter

Gather a supply of children's winter clothing: different kinds of coats, hats, mittens, gloves, boots, scarves, etc. Show the children some of the clothing you have brought and compare it to the clothing they wear to school or when they go out to play. Have the children name some of their favorite outdoor winter activities. Then, allow the children to try on some of the clothing they would have to wear to do the activities named. You may want to sing the song below and have the children actually play outside in their winter clothing.

♪ **This Is the Way We Dress in Winter Song**
Sing to the tune of "Here We Go 'Round the Mulberry Bush."

This is the way we dress in winter,
Dress in winter, dress in winter.
This is the way we dress in winter,
When the days are cold.
This is what we do in winter,
Do in winter, do in winter.
This is what we do in winter,
When we play outside.

 What Is Missing?

Put several items of winter clothing, such as mittens, a hat, boots, a coat, etc., in a row on a table. Have the children look at them. Cover the items with a large sheet or piece of cloth. Without the children seeing, reach under the sheet and remove one item. Remove the sheet and have the children look again to see if they can tell which item of clothing is missing.

Hot Cocoa and Snowman Stirring Sticks

Using a chocolate drink mix, prepare cocoa for the children to enjoy as a snack (make sure it is warm, rather than hot). To make a snowman stirring stick, give each child a plastic drinking straw or coffee stirring stick and three mini-marshmallows. The children should push the straw or stick through the marshmallows to form a snowman. Have each child dunk her snowman into her hot chocolate and enjoy.

Inside Igloos

Prior to this activity, show pictures of igloos to the class. Explain to the children that people living in the coldest parts of the world sometimes build igloos (houses made of snow). Provide a large, white sheet. Drape the sheet over several tables and chairs to form a pretend igloo. Let a few children at a time pretend to live in the igloo. Have the children in the igloo pretend to keep warm in the cold weather by staying inside.

Melting Ice Cubes

Place several ice cubes in cold water. Explain to the children that the ice cubes will melt as the water in them gets warmer. Let the children predict how long it will take the ice cubes to melt. Then, let the children check the ice cubes periodically. Remind the children to check the ice throughout the day. For example, ask, "Do you think they will melt by story time? by recess?" Let the children check at the end of each activity.

Ice Cube Painting

Fill some small bowls with water and color the water in each bowl with a different color of food coloring. Fill several plastic ice trays with the colored water and freeze overnight. Place a straw or wooden craft stick into each cube as it freezes. Pop the cubes out of the tray and give a few different colors to each child. Let the children use the ice cubes to color large sheets of white paper. Let the paintings dry and display them around the room.

🎵 I'm A Little Snowman Song
Sing to the tune of "I'm a Little Teapot."

I'm a little snowman, round and fat,
I wear a scarf, and I wear a hat.
I'm a silly snowman standing tall,
Standing tall on the snowy ground!
When the sun comes out and starts to shine,
You will see I'm hard to find!

Have the children pretend to be snowmen, first standing tall and still, then melting down into a big puddle.

Sorting and Matching Mittens/Gloves
Collect a variety of pairs of mittens and gloves. Look through your supply of left-behind mittens and provide a few that do not have mates. Put these on a table or in a pile on the floor at circle time. Have the children match the pairs. Talk about the differences between mittens and gloves. Count the pairs once they have been matched. How many mittens does it take to make a pair? How many pairs of mittens are there? How many pairs of gloves? How many do not have matches? Are there enough pairs for each child in the class to have a pair? How many more would be needed? After this activity, you may separate the pairs and keep them in a box for the children to rematch on other days.

Tracks in the Snow
After sharing books about snow and looking at pictures of the winter season, discuss with the children how they can tell when something has moved around in the snow. Show them pictures of animal tracks. You may want to share the book *The Snowy Day* by Ezra Jack Keats. Cover a table with white butcher paper. Place paper towels in several foam meat trays and add black paint. Have the children use cookie cutters, sponges, and items they can find around the room (blocks, various plastic manipulatives, etc.) to make "tracks" on the white paper.

Winter: Winter Fun

Margarine Tub Bird Feeders

Explain to the children that most birds have a harder time finding food in the winter. Ask parents to provide their child with a clean, plastic margarine tub or whipped topping tub to make a bird feeder. Punch three holes about 1" from the top of each tub, placing them an equal distance apart. Supply each child with three 1' lengths of yarn or string. Help each child tie one piece of yarn through each hole, then tie the loose ends together into a sturdy knot. As a class, fill one tub with birdseed, and hang it where it can be seen from a classroom window. Allow the children to take their feeders home. You may wish to provide each child with a plastic, resealable bag of birdseed to use with her feeder.

Bird Watching

Place a bird feeder in a tree that can be easily observed by the children. For one month keep a chart of the number of birds feeding at the feeder. Each morning let a different child be the bird watcher for the day. Ask that child to go to the window and count the birds at the feeder. Mark the number on the classroom calendar. At the end of the month, compare the number of birds sighted each day at the feeder. You may want to assign two children to be bird watchers. One will count at the beginning of the day and one will count at a later time. Write down both numbers. Compare them at the end of the day. At what time did the most birds come to the feeder?

Books to Share

First Snow: A Wordless Picture Book by Emily McCully (HarperTrophy, 1988)

The Jacket I Wear in the Snow by Shirley Neitzel (Mulberry Books, 1994)

Sadie and the Snowman by Allen Morgan (Scholastic, 1987)

The Snowy Day by Ezra Jack Keats (Scholastic, 1993)

The Mystery of the Missing Red Mitten by Steven Kellogg (Dial Books, 1994)

Spring

Spring Is Here!

Spring Headbands
Cut a strip of construction paper 3" wide and long enough to fit around each child's head. Give each child a copy of the flower pattern from page 42. Have him color and cut out the flower. Use tape to attach the flower to the headband. Tape the headband to fit around the child's head.

Wake Me Up, It's Spring!
Duplicate and cut out a copy of one of the flower patterns from page 42. Using clear tape, attach the flower to the end of a paper towel tube to make a spring wand. Have all the children pretend to be sleeping in various areas of the classroom. Explain that winter is over, the days are getting warmer, and spring is coming to the area. Choose one child to be "spring." Spring will move around the room and wake each child by tapping him with the wand. Have the children stretch and yawn as they wake from their winter slumber.

Where the Wind Blows
Give each child a craft stick. Let them tape or glue colorful streamers to the end of the stick. Take the children outside on a windy day. Have them hold up their craft sticks and watch the wind blow the streamers. Try this in several locations and have the children determine which way the wind is blowing.

Plastic Egg Sorting
Provide a collection of colored plastic eggs in a variety of sizes. Place the eggs in a basket or in a box covered with colored self-adhesive paper. Have the children sort the eggs by color and size. Encourage them to count how many eggs they have of each color and size, then count the total number of eggs.

Spring: Spring Is Here!

Five Little Bluebirds Finger Play

For this finger play, make one copy of the bird pattern strip from page 42. Cut along the lines to make five separate squares. Attach the birds to the fingertips of a work glove with hook-and-loop fasteners. Remove a bird from each finger as you read each verse of the following finger play. After the children learn the verses, let the children use the glove to do their own finger plays.

Five little bluebirds sitting in a tree.
Looked all around to see what they could see!

One little bluebird, wanted to see more.
He flew away and left only four!

Four little bluebirds high up in the tree;
One flew away, and this left three!

Three little bluebirds hiding from you.
One flew away and left only two!

Two little bluebirds playing in the sun.
One flew away, and that left one!

One little bluebird wanted to have fun.
He went to find the others, and then there were none!

Egg Carton Greenhouses

Cut off the tops of several cardboard egg cartons. Put potting soil in the sections of the egg cartons and plant seeds in each section. Cover each egg carton with a different color plastic wrap, including clear. Wrap the bottoms of the cartons in aluminum foil. Place the pans near a light source and keep them moist. Let the children predict under which color of cellophane the plants will grow best. Document what happens.

Books to Share

Chickens Aren't the Only Ones by Ruth Heller (Price Stern Sloan, 1993)

Sleepy Bear by Lydia Dabcovich (E.P. Dutton, 1993)

Wake Me in Spring by James Preller (Cartwheel Books, 1989)

Flower and Blue Bird Patterns

Spring: Spring Is Here!

42

© Carson-Dellosa CD-0217

Caterpillars, Butterflies, and Bees

Caterpillars to Butterflies
Share *The Very Hungry Caterpillar* by Eric Carle with the class. Have the children identify the different stages of a caterpillar's life: egg, caterpillar (larva), chrysalis (pupa), and butterfly. Cut the bottom of an egg carton into four sections, so that each section has three attached egg compartments. Give one section to each child, and have her turn the section upside down on a table and decorate the section with paint, markers, glitter, sequins, or stickers to resemble a caterpillar. Help her glue pipe cleaners to the end of the egg carton to represent antennae. Draw a shape resembling a pair of butterfly wings on a piece of paper (you may wish to trace the wings of the butterfly pattern from page 46). Copy one for each child onto heavy paper or construction paper and let the children color the wings. Then, cut out the wings, and help the children tape them to the egg cartons to change their caterpillars into butterflies.

Caterpillar Song
Sing to the tune of "Where is Thumbkin?" Have the children make the following motions as they sing the song.

Caterpillar, caterpillar.
Eats his fill, eats his fill.
Changes to a chrysalis, changes to a chrysalis.
Butterfly! Butterfly!

Have the children stretch from head to toe to be long, thin caterpillars. Then, have them pretend to eat leaves from trees and bushes. Each child should wrap her arms around herself and squat to be a chrysalis, and then fly around the room like a butterfly.

Paper Plate Caterpillars
Give each child four white paper plates. Have each child decorate three of the plates using crayons, markers, paint, glitter, or stickers. Have him decorate the last plate to resemble a caterpillar face. Let the child attach pipe cleaners to the face plate to resemble antennae. Attach the plates to each other in a row using brads, tape, or staples.

Cantaloupe Caterpillars
Let the children take turns using a large melon ball scoop to scoop out cantaloupe or other types of melon into balls. At snack time tell the class how many melon balls they can put on their plates to form their caterpillars. The children can use stick pretzels or short pieces of string licorice to make antennae.

We Can Fly
For this activity each child will need two 12" x 18" pieces of butcher paper. Have the children decorate the paper with markers or paint to resemble butterfly wings. Help the children cut the paper into wing-like shapes. Tape two strips of fabric or oaktag to the undecorated side of the each wing long enough for the children to slip their arms through. Then, use strips of heavy tape to attach several colorful 1'-long crepe paper streamers to the edges of the wings to emphasize movement. Have the children pull these "butterfly wings" onto their arms. Play music and have the children pretend to flap their butterfly wings, or go outside and let them "fly" in the wind.

Glittering Sun-Catching Butterflies
Give each child a copy of the butterfly pattern from page 46 on white construction paper, and help him cut out the pattern. Have the child make designs on the butterfly with glue, and then sprinkle different colors of glitter over the glue. Tape a looped piece of yarn to each butterfly's head. Hang the butterfly in a window and the glitter will catch the sunlight.

Spring: Caterpillars, Butterflies, and Bees

Butterflies or Bees

Talk with the children about the differences and similarities between bees and butterflies. Tell them that bees produce honey, while butterflies are pretty to watch. Both help pollinate flowers. Make several copies of the bee and butterfly patterns from page 46. Make a two-column graph with a large bee pattern at the top of one column and a large butterfly pattern at the top of the other. Have each child choose the pattern that represents the insect he likes the best. Have him attach the pattern in the appropriate column with sticky-tack. Let the class count the number of patterns in each column to see which insect is more popular.

Buzzing Bees

Ask one child to leave the group. Help the class choose an object to be found or identified by the child. When the child returns to the group, she must find or identify the object by walking around the room and touching things. Have the children buzz while the child tries to discover the special object. When she gets close to the object, the buzzing should get louder, until she finds the object. Play this game until each child has a chance to find an object.

Colorful Bees

Duplicate 18 copies of the bee pattern from page 46, and cut them out. Have the children color half of the bees the nine basic colors (red, yellow, blue, green, purple, orange, brown, black, and white). Write the name of one color on each of the remaining bees. Have each child match the colorful bees to the bee with the correct color word, naming the colors as he plays.

Books to Share

Charlie the Caterpillar by Dom DeLuise (Simon & Schuster, 1990)

If At First You Do Not See by Ruth Brown (Henry Holt, 1989)

The Very Hungry Caterpillar by Eric Carle (Putnam, 1986)

Where Butterflies Grow by Joanne Ryder (Puffin, 1996)

Bee and Butterfly Patterns

Spring: Caterpillars, Butterflies, and Bees

Frogs and Ducks

🄰🄱 Shape Game
Use the frog and lily pad patterns from page 51 to create a shape matching game. Copy several frog and lily pad patterns onto green construction paper, and have the children help cut them out. Separate the patterns into pairs of one frog and one lily pad. Draw a simple shape, such as a circle, square, oval, rectangle, star, triangle, diamond, or heart, onto each pair of patterns. Glue the lily pads from each pair onto the inside of one or more file folders. Laminate the folders and the frogs. Have the children match the shapes by placing the correct frog on top of the lily pad. Store the game pieces in a plastic bag glued to the back of the folders.

🄰🄱 Alphabet Lily Pad Hop
Using the pattern from page 51, copy and cut out 26 lily pads from green construction paper. Write one letter of the alphabet on each lily pad, and then laminate the lily pads. Tape the lily pads randomly to the classroom floor. As you play some lively music, have a few children pretend to be frogs and hop from lily pad to lily pad. When the music stops, tell each child to look at the letter on the lily pad on which he is standing and say the letter, or call out a letter and have the child who is standing on that letter tell you a word that starts with that letter.

Watching Tadpoles Change
If available, bring tadpoles in an aquarium and watch them change. Local pet stores may be able to help you obtain these and provide care information. Furnish a magnifying glass for the children to use as they watch the tadpoles each day. After the tadpoles have turned into frogs, find an outside area in which they can be placed.

Jump, Frog, Jump!

Place several large, plastic hoops (such as Hula Hoops®) about a foot apart on the playground. Let the children pretend to be frogs and jump from one hoop to another. Move the hoops apart and encourage the children to try again. Have the other children chant, "Jump, frog, jump!" as each child jumps.

Frogs on a Log

Provide enough banana halves, sliced lengthwise to represent logs, for each child. Have each child place her banana half on a paper plate, cut side down, and use a blunt knife or craft stick to spread a thin layer of peanut butter or softened cream cheese on top. Cut a green grape into quarters. Give each child the four green grape pieces to place on top to represent frogs on the log.

A Promise Is a Promise

Read the story *The Frog Prince* by Alix Berenzy. Use a real orange to represent the golden ball in the story. Talk to the children about what it means to make and keep a promise. Sit in a circle and roll the "golden ball" (the orange) to a child and let her tell you what kind of promise she would like to make to the others in the class or to a family member. Suggestions could include sharing toys, keeping the classroom clean, or being a friend.

Sink or Swim

Fill a water play table or a large deep pan with water. Allow the children to collect and experiment with various items from the classroom and from outside to see if they will float or sink. To make the activity more interesting, before placing the items in the water, have various children predict which items will sink and which will float. Instruct the children to give the "thumbs up" sign if they think an item will float, and the thumbs down sign if they think the items will sink. Write the predictions on a piece of chart paper. Then, let the children test their predictions.

Spring: Frogs and Ducks

Ducks in a Row

Copy and cut out eleven ducks using the duck pattern from page 51. Write a numeral from 0 to 10 (or 10 to 20, depending on how well the children can count) on each duck. Place the ducks in sequential order along the bottom of a bulletin board. Then, remove three or four ducks. Allow the children to determine which ducks are missing, then place them in the appropriate place in the row using push pins. As the children learn the numerals, remove all the ducks except for 0 and 10. Have the children place the remaining ducks in the correct sequence.

Did You Ever See a Duckling Song

Sing to the tune of "Did You Ever See a Lassie?"

Did you ever see a duckling, a duckling, a duckling?
Did you every see a duckling, swim this way and that?
He shakes and he waddles,
He's quacking and quacking.
Did you ever see a duckling swim this way and that?

Sing the song as many times as there are children, and let a different child tell the other children how he wants the ducks to move (flying, waddling, paddling, etc.) each time. As you sing the song, let the children pretend to be ducks and move around the room.

Floating Ducks

Purchase a supply of plastic ducks that will float. With a permanent marker, write a numeral or letter on the bottom of each duck. Float the ducks in the water table or in a large plastic pan of water. Have the children take turns picking up a duck and naming the letter or numeral on the bottom of the duck. As an alternative, write the children's names on the ducks. Choose one child to pick up the first duck. Then, read the name of the child on the bottom of the duck. The child whose name is chosen gets to pick the next duck.

Frog Skin and Duck Feathers

Copy a frog and duck pattern from page 51 onto white construction paper for each child. To make the frogs, provide green or brown crayons with the paper wrappers removed. Let the children take their papers outside and place them on tree trunks, then rub the crayons over the patterns to make a texture. Have the children cut out the pattern. To create ducks, have the children cut out the pattern and sponge paint it with brown and yellow paint, or have them glue on craft feathers. These patterns can be used with the pond bulletin board below.

Finger Paint Pond

Cover a table top with finger-paint paper or butcher paper. Drop blue paint on the paper with a tablespoon and allow the children to finger paint a pond. When the paint has dried, cut out the pond and attach it to a bulletin board or a wall. Help the children cut out copies of the frog, duck, and lily pad patterns from page 51. Have the children color the patterns and tape them to the pond. They may also enjoy coloring grass, turtles, cattails, fish, or other items in and around the pond.

Books to Share

Frogs, Toads, Lizards, and Salamanders by Nancy Winslow Parker and Joan Richards Wright (Mulberry Books, 1996)

In the Small, Small Pond by Denise Fleming (Henry Holt & Co., 1993)

Jump, Frog, Jump by Robert Kalan (Mulberry Books, 1989)

Make Way for Ducklings by Robert McCloskey (Viking, 1976)

The Frog Prince by Alix Berenzy (Henry Holt, 1991)

Spring: Frogs and Ducks

Lily Pad, Duck, and Frog Patterns

© Carson-Dellosa CD-0217   51   *Spring: Frogs and Ducks*

Rainy Weather

Walking in the Rain
Take the children outside and pretend to walk in the rain. Talk about what you might see, how it might feel, and what you might hear. Use descriptive words and allow the children to hold umbrellas and pretend to be jumping over or splashing through a puddle, walking through wet grass, tiptoeing through rain, and drying off when they come inside. If possible, provide umbrellas, boots, and rain coats and allow the children to use them during free play time. As an alternative, you may wish to plan a rainy day walk. Have the children dress appropriately and take a walk outside.

Rain, Rain Falling Down Song
Sing to the tune of "Row, Row, Row Your Boat."

Rain, rain, falling down,
Falling to the ground.
Splashing, splashing, splashing down,
What a happy sound!

Rain Drops Change Things
Let the children use paintbrushes to drop water on different colors of construction paper. Have the children notice the effect the "rain" drops have on the paper. Gather various items, such as sponges, cotton balls, pieces of fabric, a teaspoon of flour or sugar, building blocks, etc., and encourage the children to predict which objects will absorb raindrops. Invite the children to test their predictions by using a paintbrush to drop water on each item.

Spring: Rainy Weather

Clouds
Share the book *It Looked Like Spilt Milk* by Charles Shaw. Let the children look at the pictures in the book and tell you what each picture looks like. Give each child a piece of white paper, and ask her to tear it into any shape she wishes. Have her glue this shape onto dark blue paper. Then ask each of the children to show his torn picture and let the class tell what they think the "clouds" look like.

Thunder and Storms
Talk to the children about lightning and the sound of thunder. Let them share any fears they have. Share the book *Thunder Cake* by Patricia Polacco. Tell the children to stomp their feet every time thunder is mentioned in the story. You may want to use the recipe in the back of the book and let the children help bake Grandma's Thunder Cake.

Rainbows
Create a rainbow in your classroom by filling a glass with water. Place a small mirror in the glass. Place the glass on the windowsill on a white piece of construction paper. When the sun shines through the water onto the mirror, a rainbow should appear on the paper. You may have to move the mirror around in the glass until the sunlight is shining directly on it.

Art Rainbows
Have the children make their own rainbows using colored markers or crayons. Help the children cut out their rainbows, then glue cotton balls on both ends of their rainbows to represent clouds. Display these around the room.

Books to Share
It Looked Like Spilt Milk by Charles G. Shaw (HarperTrophy, 1988)

Planting a Rainbow by Lois Ehlert (Harcourt Brace, 1992)

Thunder Cake by Patricia Polacco (Paper Star, 1997)

Umbrella by Taro Yashima (Puffin, 1985)

Summer

Water, Shells, and Sand

Ocean in a Bottle
Give each child a clear, plastic soda bottle which has been washed and has the labels removed. Cover a table with newspapers. Let each child use a funnel to pour a cup of sand into her bottle. She should then fill the rest of the bottle with water and add a few drops of blue food coloring. Encourage her to add aquarium rocks, craft shells, or small seashells, then replace the lid tightly. Let each child decorate the outside of the bottle with fish stickers or markers. Have each child shake her bottle to make ocean waves.

Water Table Toss Game
Cut the sections of a foam egg carton apart. Float the sections in the water table or in a shallow, plastic tub placed on the ground outside. Give the children a supply of pennies. Ask them to predict how many pennies one section of the carton can hold before sinking. Have the children add pennies to an egg carton section until it sinks.

How Much Will It Hold?
You will need a measuring cup, a funnel, and a large clear plastic container or 2-liter soft drink bottle. Let the children estimate how many cups of water it will take to fill the large container. Then, have the children measure water by the cupful and count the cups as they fill the container.

[handwritten: Ocean in a Bottle with Whales?]

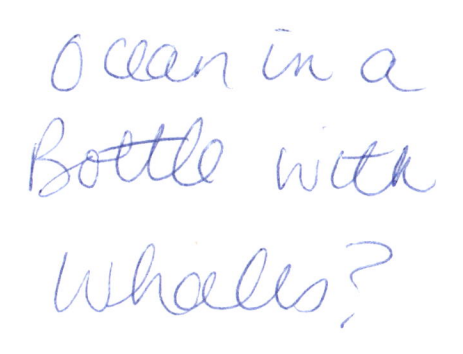

...me Amount?

...s that hold the same amount (for example, eight
...g cup; a coffee mug; a baby bottle; a tall, plastic
...foam cup. Place the items on the table and ask the
...hey think will hold the same amount. Using an eight
...a child or several children fill each container with
...all of the containers are full, have the children talk
...s hold the same amount. For example, some con-
...other are short and wide.

...designs on waxed paper. Let them sprinkle sand
...cess sand and allow the design to dry overnight.
...ut out their designs around the outer edge of the
...designs can be hung from a mobile or by a window.

Sea Shore Design

Give each child a piece of blue construction paper. Have each child draw boats, fish, or other sea animals on the top half of the paper. Then, let her apply glue to the bottom half of the paper and then sprinkle it with sand. Let it dry, then let her glue small shells or aquarium rocks on top of the sand.

Sand Table Search

Hide a collection of large, colorful beads in the sand table or playground sandbox. Have the children go on a "treasure hunt" to look for the beads. When all of the beads have been found, have the children sort them by shape or color.

Move Like Crabs

Tell the children sit on the floor, then have them lean back on their hands and bend their knees, lifting themselves off the floor. They will be "walking" on their hands and feet. Have them walk sideways like crabs.

"Down by the Sea" Snack

Start preparing blueberry gelatin before beginning this activity. Purchase graham cracker crumbs or have the children prepare their own by crushing graham crackers in a plastic bag. Let each child fill a clear plastic cup or plastic resealable bag halfway full with the crumbs. Pour some of the blueberry gelatin over the crumbs. The children may want to add fish-shaped gummy candies. Place the cups in the refrigerator until the gelatin finishes congealing then allow the children to enjoy the snack.

"Sharing" Fish

Discuss the importance of sharing with the class. If possible, share the book *The Rainbow Fish* by Marcus Pfister. Copy the large fish pattern from page 58 for each child. Have each child put scales on his fish by adding a thin layer of white glue with a paintbrush and attaching 1" colored tissue paper squares. Add to the fun by cutting many 1" scales from aluminum foil, then scattering these around the room. Go on a treasure hunt with the children to locate the silver scales. Provide a container in which the children can place all the scales they find. Let the children each have some silver scales from the container to glue on their fish. Remind them that they shared by putting all of the silver scales into one container.

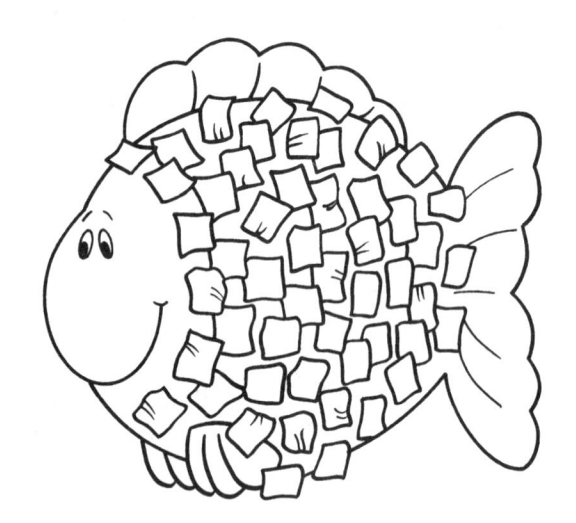

Plenty of Shells

Bring a variety of sea shells to class (these can be purchased at many craft stores). You may also want to bring sea animals that have dried out, such as starfish, sand dollars, or sea urchins. If possible, bring a conch shell to class. Let the children pass the conch shell around and listen to the opening. Have them describe what they hear. Place all of the shells in a gift box or lid lined with a dish towel or bath towel. Keep the shells in the science center for children to examine.

Summer: Water, Shells, and Sand

✏️ Hermit Crab Listening Assignment

Plan to share the book *A House for Hermit Crab* by Eric Carle. Give each child a lunch bag or resealable plastic bag containing fish-shaped crackers or gummy fish candies and a napkin or small paper plate. Tell the children you are going to give them a listening assignment. Instruct the children to listen carefully and take a fish out of the bag every time Hermit Crab adds something new to his shell. Count the fish they have laid out, and compare the number to the things Hermit Crab added to his shell. Go back and look through the book and discuss the story and the things Hermit did. After the activity, let the children eat the fish for a snack, or take them home to enjoy.

✏️ School of Fish

Cut several pieces of construction paper into 4" x 6" rectangles. On each square, write the name of an ocean animal or fish, such as *octopus, jellyfish, crab, shark, whale, dolphin*, etc. Draw a picture or use a sticker representing the word on the other side of the shape. Laminate the rectangles and place them in a small net. Sit with the children and pull out one of the cards. Show the children the word and picture and say a sentence using that word. Pass the net around and as a child takes out a card, read the word to her and encourage her to say a sentence using the new word.

📖 Books to Share

A House for Hermit Crab by Eric Carle (Simon & Schuster, 1988)

The Rainbow Fish by Marcus Pfister (North South Books, 1992)

Swimmy by Leo Lionni (Knopf, 1992)

Fish Patterns

Summer: Water, Shells, and Sand 58 © Carson-Dellosa CD-0217

Watermelons

Farmer's Market Field Trip
Plan a field trip to a farmer's market or grocery store (make arrangements with the manager first) so that the children can choose a watermelon to have as a snack. If possible, spread a blanket on the ground at a park or in the playground, pass out napkins and paper plates, and let the children sit on the blanket to eat the watermelon. Remove the seeds and provide salt and sugar for the children to sprinkle on their watermelon slices. Also provide spoons and melon ball scoopers for the children to use to sample their watermelons.

Melon Comparison
Bring in several different types of melons, such as canteloupe, honeydew, yellow-fleshed or seedless watermelon, etc., to compare with a regular watermelon. Compare the shape and texture of the outsides of the melons, then cut them open and look at the insides. How are they alike? How are they different?

Guess the Circumference
Bring a watermelon to class. Cut three lengths of yarn, making sure that one is the circumference of the watermelon, one is several inches shorter, and one is several inches longer. Have the children sit in a circle. Place the watermelon and yarn on the floor. Have the children take turns guessing which length of yarn will fit around the watermelon. Allow volunteers to wrap the yarn around the watermelon. Measure the lengths of yarn against a yardstick.

Sorting Seeds
Provide seeds from several types of melons. Draw a picture of each kind of melon and attach its seed with tape to the end of a craft stick. Tape the sticks to clear plastic cups, and have the children sort the right kind of seed into each cup.

Watermelon Pictures

Give each child one half of a paper plate. Write the child's name and a numeral from 1 through 10 on the back of each child's plate half. Furnish green and red paint and brushes. Have the children paint the round edge of their plates green and the rest of the plate red to resemble a slice of watermelon. When the plates are dry, have the children look at the numerals on the backs of their plates and glue that many real watermelon seeds to the painted side of their plates.

Matching Seed Numbers

Make 22 copies of the watermelon pattern from page 61. With a black marker, write a different numeral from 0 through 10 on eleven of the slices. On the other eleven paper slices glue a matching number of watermelon seeds for each number. Have a child count the seeds on each slice, and then place the slice with the corresponding numeral beside it.

Comparing Seeds

Bring apple and watermelon seeds to class, and ask the children to describe the differences in color, shape, and size. If possible, bring in other types of seeds that are very different, such as peach or avocado pits. Talk about the similarities and differences between what happens to the seeds when they are planted. One produces a tree and the other a vine, and one produces a much larger fruit than the other. You may wish to bring in a picture of an apple tree and a watermelon vine.

Books to Share

Blueberries for Sal by Robert McCloskey (Viking, 1978)

Growing Colors by Bruce McMillan (Lothrop, Lee and Shepard Books, 1988)

Jamberry by Bruce Degen (HarperCollins, 1990)

The Little Mouse, Red Ripe Strawberry and Big Hungry Bear by Audrey and Don Wood (Child's Play Singapore, 1989)

Watermelon Patterns

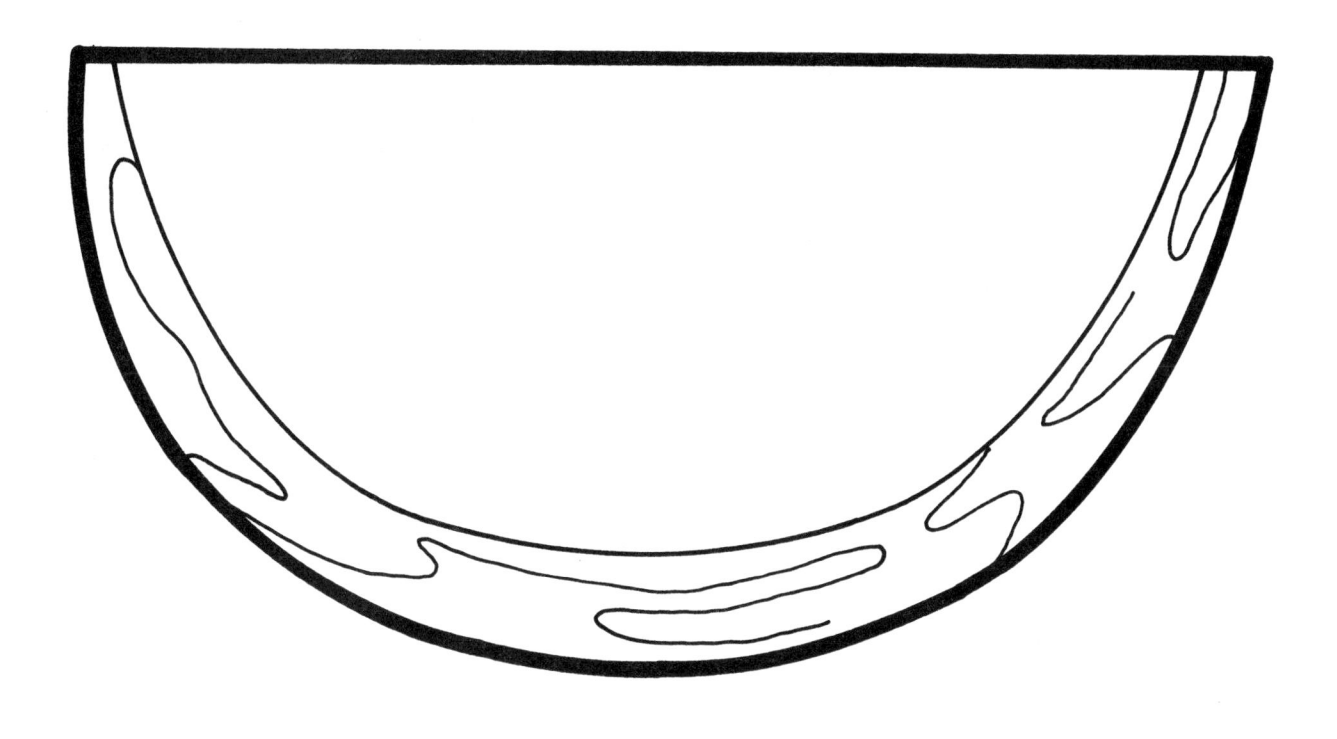

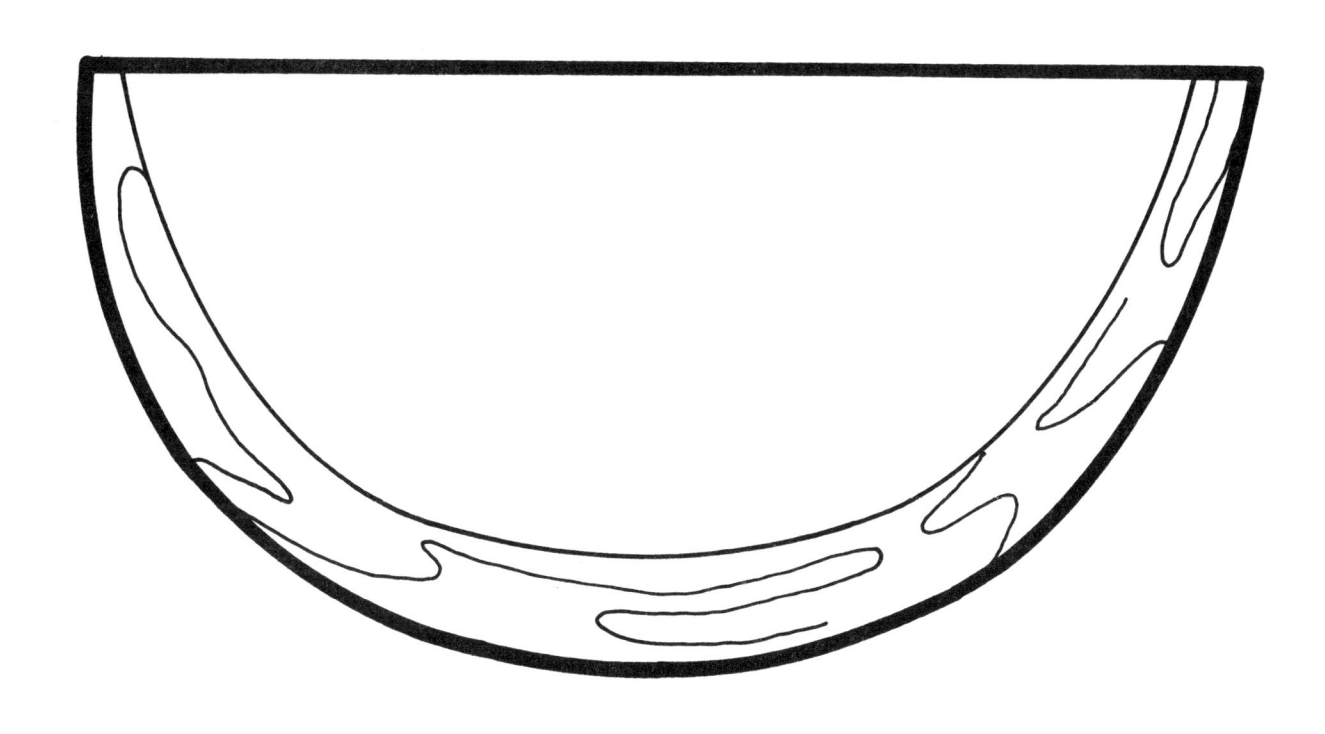

61

Summer: Watermelons

Picnic

Packing a Picnic Basket

Make a copy of the picnic basket from page 64 for each child on brown construction paper. Have him cut out the basket. Provide a number of old magazines. Let the children cut or tear out pictures from the magazines of their favorite foods and glue or tape them to the basket. Post the baskets on a bulletin board titled, "Let's Go on a Picnic!"

Waltzing Matilda

If possible, share A. B. Patterson's book *Waltzing Matilda*. Read the title and ask the children what they think it means. A *matilda* is a backpack, and to *waltz* with it actually means to walk with your belongings in your backpack. Since this book is from Australia, there may be some words that are unfamiliar to the class. You may want to use the glossary in the back to help the class learn and repeat some of the new words. You may also want to show them Australia on a globe.

Making Matildas

Ask parents to furnish two medium or large brown paper grocery bags for their child. Let the child decorate his bag using paint, markers, or crayons. Write each child's name on his bag. Cut two 4"-wide strips which are the length of the other bag. Help the child tape the ends of each strip together to form two large loops. Glue or tape each loop to the top of the decorated bag to form straps. Have the child put his lunch in his matilda, and carefully slide the loops over his arms and onto his shoulders. Allow all of the children to walk around the room or the playground, and then enjoy their lunches.

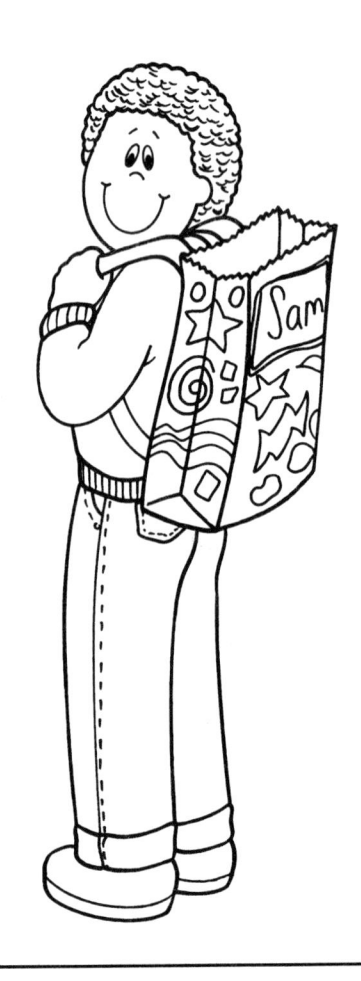

Summer: Picnic

Picnic Hamburgers

Give each child a paper plate and two circles, about 4" in diameter, cut from brown construction paper. Have each child place one circle (hamburger bun) on the plate. Provide construction paper scraps and scissors. Let the children create hamburgers using the scrap paper to make various toppings to place on the bun. For example, a black circle could represent a hamburger patty, a yellow square could represent cheese, torn green paper could represent lettuce, etc. Have the children stack the ingredients to the hamburger buns. Let the children draw sesame seeds on top of the bun. Then, put each child's hamburger pieces in a resealable plastic bag and let her take the pieces home to reconstruct the hamburger for her parents.

Ground Jump Rope

For an after-picnic game, place two jump ropes parallel on the ground close together. Have the children line up and take turns jumping over the ropes. When it is the first child's turn again, place the ropes a little further apart. Keep making the distance between the two ropes greater until it becomes difficult to clear them without stepping on the ropes The last child to clear both ropes is the winner.

Books to Share

The Car Trip by Helen Oxenbury (Puffin, 1994)

Waltzing Matilda by A. B. Paterson (Australia in Print, 1989)

Picnic Basket Pattern

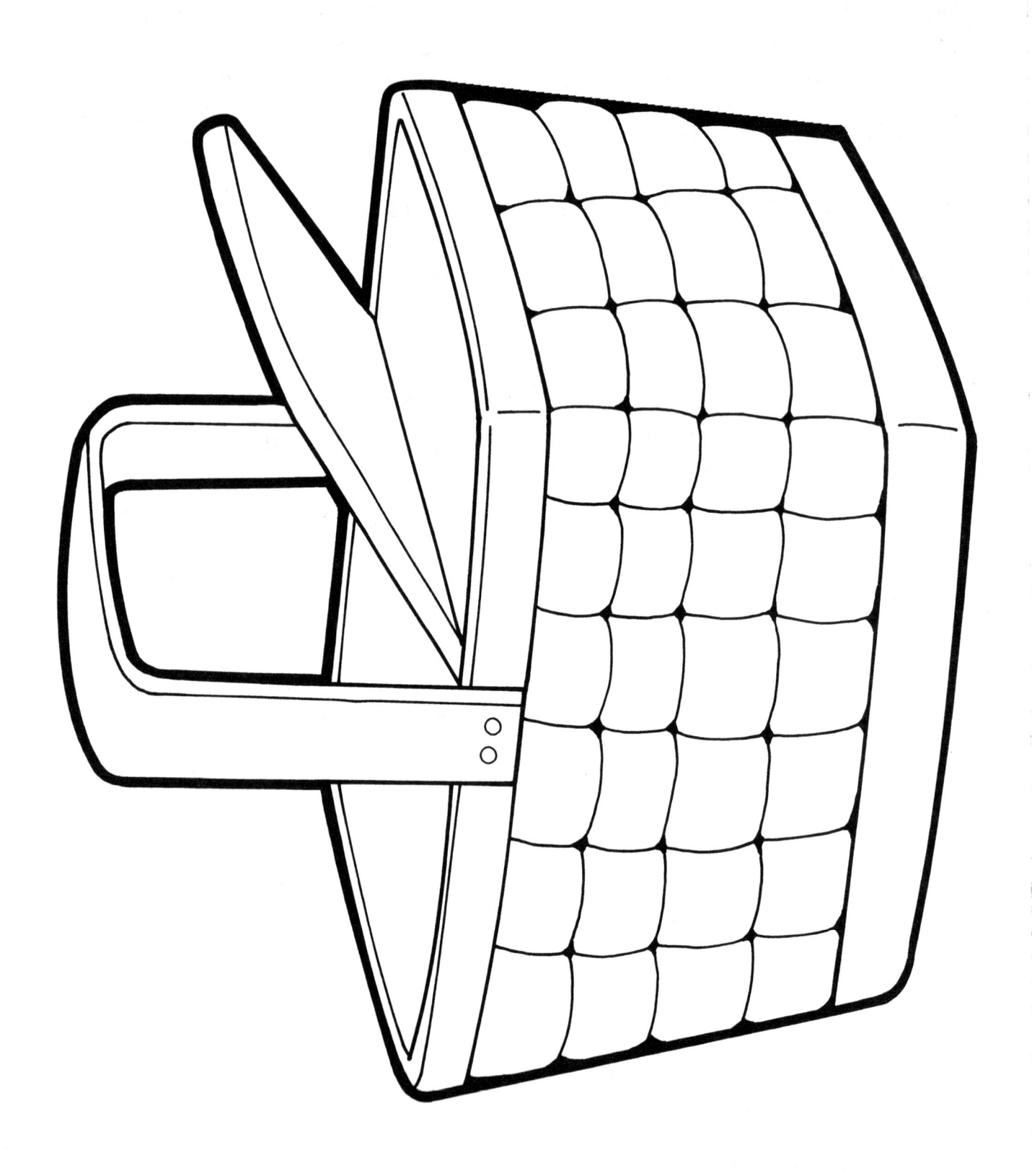

Summer: Picnic